TX  1-623-482

# ❀ SEEDBURSTS ❀

For those whose
life journeys
matter to themselves
and others

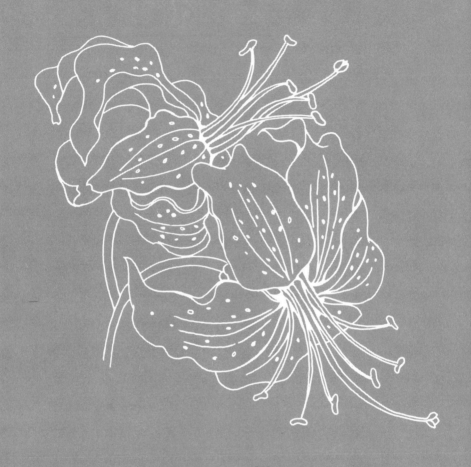

# SEED BURSTS

## Spiritual Aphorisms for Life Change

by

## Strephon Kaplan Williams

Journey Press
Berkeley, California

Copyright © 1984 by Strephon Kaplan Williams
All rights reserved
Published by Journey Press
P.O. Box 9036, Berkeley, California 94709
Designed by Strephon Williams
Cover design by Chris Molé
Composition by Vera Allen Composition
Printed and bound by McNaughten and Gunn

ISBN 0-918572-27-4
Manufactured in the United States of America
Library of Congress card catalogue number

BF 637,C5W55 1984

First edition
Printing 9 8 7 6 5 4 3 2 1

# ❁ CONTENTS ❁

# ❀ DEDICATION ❀

I look back on my life during the years of intimacy when these aphorisms and principles were being formulated and I think of one primarily from among the friends I had.

Each of the principles we used with each other, weaving them in through loving, tears, anger, caring, meaning, and accomplishment.

She was to me as one who knew not just my way, but the way, a subtle companion able to move me through nuances of soul. We reached out for each other and met often on the periphery of consciousness. We were bold in our demands of life and ever insightful in the struggle.

And what was our accomplishment? To never leave the field of battle whether it be the lovemaking bed, a creative work together, the intense conversation, the angry issues, a point of philosophy, the other folks in our lives, never leaving any of these forever, but resolving them in such a way that we could both move on in life.

She was like one in beauty every part of her a woman who took me in and loved, yet never yielding in the melting warmth a sense of her own destiny and of soul.

And when she must break from me she did. And when I must take another path, I went. And we were to meet again as deep friends and sometimes lovers, understandable to ourselves if to no other.

I was a man to her, teacher, bringer of life from the masculine end. I was softened, challenged and affirmed. I was renewed. Pretty in her own way, I loved her firm body that had the dancer's life in it, the kisses were often sweet and intense in their giving. We moved through realms of love together, and I thank you, my companion of those years. We are a part of each other forever.

—Strephon

# ❖ An Invitation ❖

*Seedbursts! The title occurred to me or one of our group
a few years ago when I was first assembling this material.*

*What you will find here are spiritual aphorisms or
sayings which attempt to describe universal laws of
meaning as they act in everyday life.*

*"To become conscious we must act" is a statement
about ourselves and life which says it is not enough to
simply reflect on things or meditate all day to know
reality and it's manifestations. One gets far more
nourishment, usually, from eating food than from merely
thinking about it. And in like manner, it is not food
which makes us hungry, but the thinking about it which
does.*

*"Out of action must come reflection in order to
become conscious." Another spiritual aphorism, but this
time we have stated it as a reversal of content and as the
other half of the process.*

*Almost all of these aphorisms came to me in working
with people using my own form of a Jungian growth
process. We have had a community for several years in
which we practice dreamwork, ceremony, and working*

with other aspects of inner and outer individuation. The sayings would be written down on little colored cards and placed in a basket. Then at the end of dream session participants would be invited to synchronisticly choose a card and, without expectation, work with the aphorism for relevance in their lives right then. Often the statements would be startling and directly related to a person's issue.

I would certainly like to affirm first Terran Harcort Daily, my full time companion of the years 1977-1982, whose statement on spending time wisely is in this book. Harriet Jasik Skibbins, my professional colleague during many of those same years, also has my deep gratitude. Anna Joyce is my present editor and director of Journey Press, and a great help in getting the material out. My thanks go finally to the many others who have been journeyers along the way as we have lent each other pieces of our lives and developed a sense of community and life lived richly.

Now is the present time for the life of this book. It is to each of us who are the readers to share in whatever meaning can come through working with this material. Out of community and into community again.

As the writer as well as one who lives what is recorded here, I am the vehicle. But this book is really for each reader who responds. We invite you to let these sayings affect you. Each one is followed by questions as a way of focusing what gets evoked. You will have reactions.

*Things may fall into place here and there. You may also be startled. You may also disagree. You are invited to restate the aphorisms in different words. Some of them can also be said in reverse and evoke meaning.*

*What we also have here is a whole course in journalwork or meditation. You can do things such as taking one statement a day and working with it. Perhaps you would choose to set aside fifteen or more minutes upon awaking to write upon or meditate upon a statement? Since these are principles which challenge attitudes and deal with consciousness, such work may affect your whole day and eventually how you are or are not living life. Or you might choose to work with a statement in the transition moments before bedtime. Why not use this material as a basis for discussion in a group or among friends? I would like nothing better than to know once in awhile the book is being whipped out, read, and discussed during a fine dinner together.*

*To be spiritual is to explore the meaning in life. We do not need drugs or other outside stimulants to tune into the core realities of life. We need, rather, activity and dedication to look deeper than the surface of things inside ourselves and in others, and in life situations also. Healing can come more often from intunement with life as it really is than by attempting to cleanse ourselves of the imperfections and terrors of life.*

*But all this is up to you and how you choose. I let the book go now. My work with it is done, at least for the moment. Whether it reaches a silent or a full world is up to all of us.*

*"From seed into air into soil into growth into fullness into harvest into essence I now welcome life!"*

—*Strephon Kaplan Williams*
*April 2, 1984, Berkeley, California*

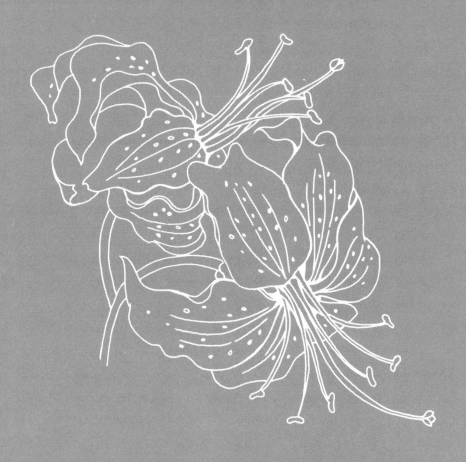

# ❁ Relationship ❁

So much of our waking thoughts and even our dreams are involved with relationships. Love relationships often evoke the most energy. Just as important are family relationships and various friendships. Yet anyone we interact with is part of a relationship, our enemies, those we work for, those we have authority over.

Every relationship is ultimately with oneself. The others? Yes, they are part of our lives in various ways, but what they arouse is within. We deal with the inner aspects of ourselves evoked by relationship.

And so when we are old and ready to die what are our memories? What we have essentially is only ourselves. What have I learned from each of my relationships? How have I grown and realized myself because of each one of you?

I am never entirely alone when I have myself.

Every relationship
is
preparation
for the real one

What is the real relationship
for you?

To love who I am
                    love
who I can become



How open am I to being loved
for who I can become?

The instincts
rule
       what has not
been made
           conscious

What is an example of this
from your own life?

## ❀ OUR ENEMIES ❀

Our enemies are
our
best friends

In what ways do you dislike
this statement?

How might it still
be true in life?

## ❀ HEALING THE PAST ❀

The way to
heal the past
is to live
fully
in the present

Describe some ways you
are stuck in the past.

Then translate a problem
into a creative action you
will do in the present.

There is nothing
to live over
        It could not
        have been otherwise

What do you still strongly wish
could have been different?

How might you choose now to
accept what happened to you
as a meaningful necessity?

There is no
right relationship
There is only
relationship

What kind of acceptance is required
of you to take this into yourself?

# ❀ THE IDEAL RELATIONSHIP ❀

The ideal
　　　　　relationship
is
the present one

How might your present relationship
be ideal for both of you right now?

What are some of the major things
you have left to learn from your
present relationship?

Relationship
is growing

                                                                  separately

together




                        How would you express this
                        as an image?

## ❀ REJECTION ❀

Nobody can
reject us
    We reject
only ourselves

If I really accepted myself
what might I be like?

# ❀ ADVERSARIES ❀

We do not choose
our adversaries
We choose to deal with them

And what adversaries are you avoiding
or dealing with this week?

Every relationship

                   is ultimately

with
myself

What kind of freedom
might living this principle
create in my relationships?

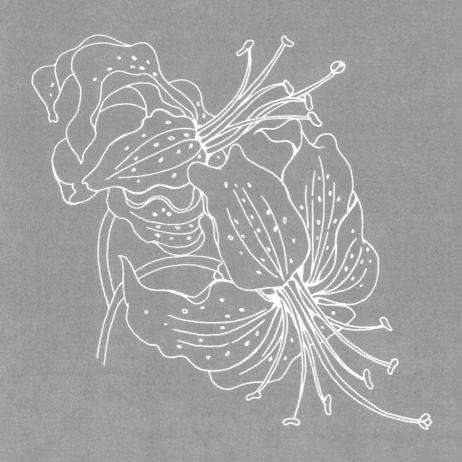

# ❖ Love ❖

Love is such a universal word and experience that it is easy to lose ourselves in what it actually means. What is love? Ask rather, how can I love more? What is the place of love in my life? How does love affect me? And how do I affect the universal stream of love?

I will not here define love. Love can only be defined by experience. I must have experience, lots of it. And then do I also go to my alone place, my journal, my solitude, and reflect on my experience of love.

I choose to discover and live fully the principles which give life its meaning. I go forward. I seek. I unite with my beloved for consciousness sake. I love.

To be loved
we must love

Quite a switch from an
"I need to be loved" attitude.

Resay the statement in your own words.
How can you become more loving?

# ❀ THE IDEAL LOVE ❀

The ideal love
is reality

Yes, describe how this reality principle
can apply to your love life.

Not who
but how
I love


And how do you love?

What we cannot
possess
we can love

Say this in your own words.

Then say or write the opposite.

Is this a truth which works both ways?

Love hurts
        that which
it most heals


Now for the hard part!

Are you able to include hurting someone
as part of your love life?

Are you willing to be hurt also
as part of risking?

And are you willing to work at healing
any wounds which come up as a natural
part of loving?

# ❀ LOVE UNITES ❀

Love unites
    what it also
        splits apart

The splitting apart is shattering.
We like the uniting!

How do these dynamics work
in your love life?

That love
which
transforms
anger
is love


And how can your love express
anger, yet transform it?

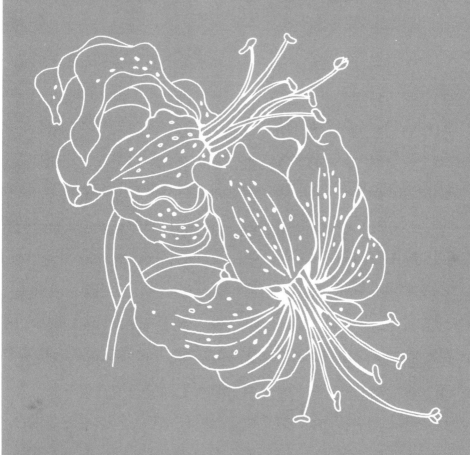

# ❀ Choice ❀

*Choice is such a beautiful and decisive word. Hear the clear call of a bell struck just once. In each moment, through choice, we are summoned to our destiny.*

Choice is
the one
absolute

Explain how this might work when
you really choose.

What is your one absolute?

## ❀ DESTINY ❀

Through choice
we turn fate
into

                         destiny

What for you is the difference
between fate and destiny?

## ❀ TO LIVE BY DYING ❀

> Each choice
>       is
> the choice
>      to live by
> dying

How do we die in choosing?

How do we live in choosing?

You must go
through your

"no's"

to get to

your "yes"



Do you tend to say "yes" more than "no",
or "no" more than "yes" in life?

How willing are you to say "no"?

How willing are you to accept a "no" coming your
way?

## ❀ MISTAKES ❀

There are no

                                     mistakes

Only choices and their
consequences

You probably do not accept this yet.

Write about a "mistake" you have
not yet accepted.

Rewrite the "mistake" as a choice
and its  consequences.

We choose "yes"
to one thing
by choosing "no"
         to all that would
         oppose it


What is there to learn about choice
from this saying?

# ❀ YOUR ULTIMATE CHOICE ❀

The context
for choice
is
the more ultimate

                                             choice

What is your context for choice?

What are you really choosing for
in each specific choice you make?

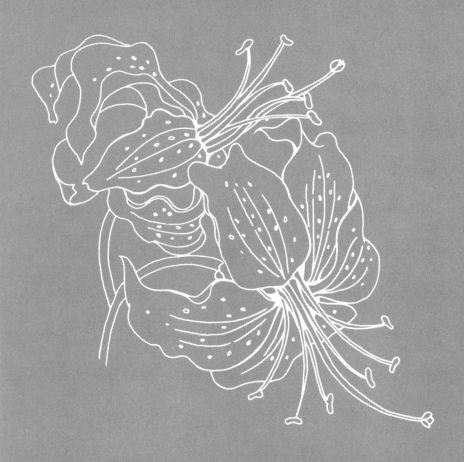

# ❀ *Person* ❀

To become a person is to devote a part of each day to self-reflection, integration and wholeness within ourselves.

See clearly the issue. The world calls us so completely that we may become stuck in spending most of our time doing outer tasks while neglecting ourselves. Take time and creativity for yourself, so that when you look back upon yourself and your life you will see not just the houses you have built or the children you have parented. You will see also yourself developing through the years, more and more full of the wholeness and destiny of being a person.

We defend
ourselves against
          that which we are
unable or unwilling
to process

What is the key here?

If you could really deal effectively with
that which you fear, what might happen?

## ❀ BLAMING ❀

We
            blame others because
we are really
            blaming ourselves

And how do you sometimes do this?

Write about it without blaming yourself.

## ❀ PLAY ❀

Play
frees
us

        from

           ourselves

Play with these words to
create several meanings.

# ❀ INFLATION ❀

Inflation
is identification
with the next
potential

.

Still, what must we do to cure ourselves
when we get in that puffed up state?

How about hard work and grounding
in the real world?

Fear
is
the
ego's
dark
ecstasy

Fear has its thrills.

What does fear have to teach
your ego, your choice-maker and
conscious side of yourself?

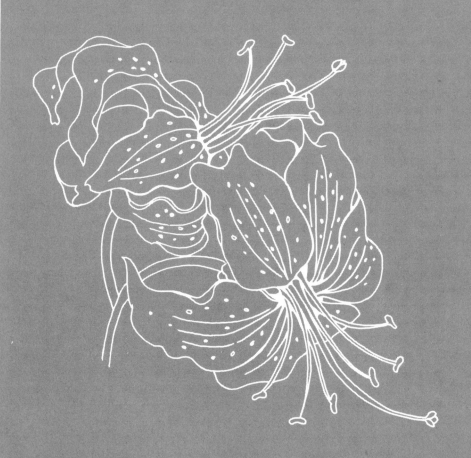

# ❋ The Journey ❋

To journey is to live life not only at the surface of things but deep down within the core, the soul of the event and the soul within oneself. We parallel the outer life with the inner life. We continually unite inner and outer. We get our principles straight. We choose strongly at the destiny points. We do not look back. We accept and go with superior forces. We seek to manifest the meaning in each moment of our lives. We seek wholeness in whatever we do. We choose to follow the guiding sources of our lives. We are ready.

There is no
        future for
        those who do not
        let go of the
past

Incredible how much we all hold on
to our yesterdays. Choose today to
really let go of one thing from your
past.

The
    journey
        greets
            me
                each day I choose
    the meaning in my
        life

Meaning is the relation between things.

What have I chosen today for meaning
in my life?

To journey
go
where
the
fear
is


Ah, the fear! Is that what is at
the end of my rainbow?

Until you
get there

be where

you are

What?

## ❀ THE ESSENTIAL ❀

To journey
is to take
    only what is
    essential
    through life

What attitudes, values, hopes, problems,
etc. are you carrying around which are
not essential to your life?

Define the essence of one of these and
let the superfluous go.

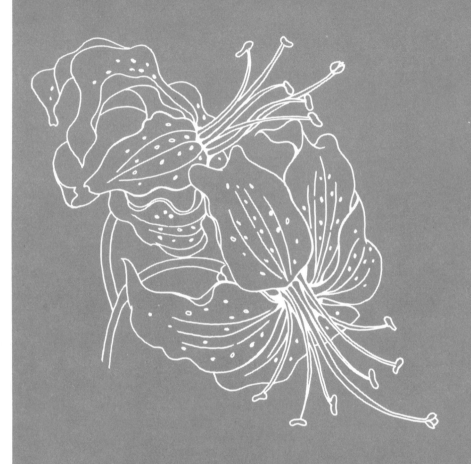

# ❋ Consciousness ❋

Each one of us has ultimately the choice as to what we do with our lives. And here we get into the meaning of life. In the seedburst does the seed have a sense of what it can become and choose it? Yes and no. We and the seed are predetermined. We have to do certain things in life or become a fatality. Yet within the context of what we have to deal with to survive and flourish we have choice.

I have the choice to live or die in so many little and big ways. I have a choice as to how I relate to whatever happens to me. I have a choice in each moment whether to realize its potential or not.

And in order to choose effectively I must have consciousness. I must become as aware as possible as to what is actually happening in myself and the situation. I must become aware of the possible values and meanings. And then out of that awareness I act. Awareness without action to test and fulfill that awareness is ungrounded. That which does not purposefully change things is but an image of the real.

May my consciousness of what is grow and prosper. And may I use it well to manifest the meaning in my reality.

More important
than what
happens to us
is what we
learn from it

Why not stop complaining
then, and learn from
whatever comes your way?

# ❀ TO PROCESS ❀

To process
is
everything

Live this principle for a week
and see what happens to you.

May your light          reveal
what
        it most hides

Yes, we can hide behind our light.

Describe how.

# ❦ CONSCIOUSNESS ❦

Consciousness

is

awareness

plus

appropriate
action

Why do awareness and appropriate
action go together?

Break the aphorism down into a
practice which you can use in your life

# ❀ VALUES ❀

Values
                    are
        attitudes
consciously
        realized


Attitudes, unlike values, are
unconscious contexts within which
we make our choices.

Take a recent choice you have
not liked and list three
possible attitudes underlying
why you made that choice.

Then substitute one value you
would have liked instead to
have used as a base for choosing.

There is
no knowledge
without
commitment

What does this mean to you?

What kind of knowledge
requires commitment?

# ❀ WISDOM ❀

Wisdom is
the distilled essence
of
experience

What is your way of coming
to the essence of what life,
or an experience, is all about?

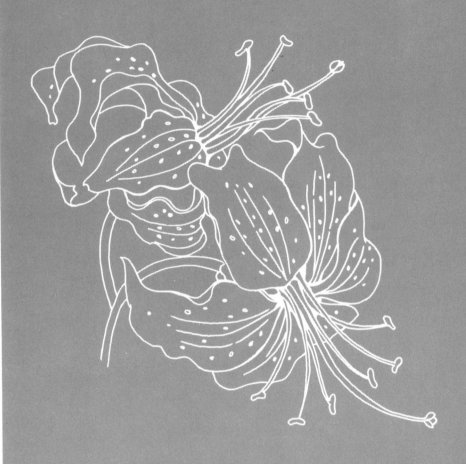

# ❄ Healing ❄

Nothing is more needed in the world and in our own lives than healing. When I think of healing I think of bringing resolution. We desire healing, not just for sickness, but as a practice in each moment.

What am I helping resolve inside myself right now by reading these words? Perhaps I am feeling uneasy or frustrated and don't know what to do? Perhaps I have not got my principles straight?

Resolution then is necessary. We have innumerable problems every day. How shall we resolve them? Sometimes by decisively ending an intolerable condition? Sometimes through release or actualization of a fresh potential? Sometimes by evoking a new unity out of the alternatives in the conflict?

We go to the wounds, the difficulties, the conflicts, and deal with them, confident that healing, that a creative solution, is always possible in any circumstance.

Healing has got to be the greatest beauty on earth.

Reality
    is
        a
great
        healer

The cure when things do not go
right is what?

# ❀ GUILT ❀

Guilt is
unresolved tension
between
opposites

What do you presently feel
guilty about?

List the opposites involved and
the tensions they cause.

Then choose as decisively as
you can a new possibility to
help resolve the tension.

# ❀ THE GREATEST COMPLAINERS ❀

The self-imprisoning
are
the greatest
complainers


What might happen in your life
if you consciously chose to stop
complaining?

## ❀ EVERY COMPULSION ❀

Behind every
compulsion
lurks a god

Whom do I unconsciously serve?

Go where

the energy is

there

you will find

wholeness

Use this principle with a current
difficult choice and describe
what happens for you.

Healing can
only come after

the plunge

to woundedness


What feelings are evoked
by this statement?

# ❀ THE CURE ❀

The cure
is
the impossible
task

It's in many of the hero myths to do
the impossible task before gaining the goal.

When you feel hardput, then do what is
needed, even if it seems overwhelming.

Help may come in from the other side.

Decide on an impossible task which
needs doing right now.

# ❀ PRAYER ❀

Prayer is
    the recognition
        of evil
  within
      the heart
of the universe

Why do we need to pray?

And what is evil in your everyday life?

Matter is

holy

You cannot leap

into the air

unless you are

on the ground

What does this say about yourself?

## ❀ BECOMING WHOLE ❀

We heal
by
becoming
whole

What personal statement will I make
here about my own healing?

# ❀ The Dark Side ❀

Yes, the dark side. Too long has humanity fled from the darkness, the suffering, the evil in the world. You will not, from your ego's point of view, enjoy, even relish, dealing with the dark side, the shadow side of life. But deal with it you must.

There is an unrelenting law to existence which can be stated as, what you flee from in life will overtake you in the end. What you seek to avoid you will nourish with your fears.

How much better then to confront the agony and imperfections of life and deal with them with the subtlety and compassion of a spiritual warrior.

I happen to feel and to operate my life on the principle that much wealth resides in what we would first reject. We do not usually get tested nearly as much by the good things of life as by the bad.

The mystical warrior seeks adversity rather than flees from it. Nowhere, repeat, nowhere is the struggle greater, is courage and all the virtues more necessary, than in the daily encounter with the dark side.

# ❀ OUR DEMONS ❀

Our demons
are what
we avoid
making conscious

Yes, write about a demon in your
life right now and how you might
be avoiding making it conscious?

# ❀ RESISTING ❀

Resisting
something
        makes
              it
        evil

What is the opposite
of resisting for you?

 ANGER ❀

We are only
          angry at ourselves

Take a recent example of when you
were angry at someone and see it as
really being angry at yourself.

How were you not being conscious
enough, or not self-protective enough?

How is self-protection different
from defensiveness?

# ❋ THE GREATEST DARKNESS ❋

Fleeing to the
light is the
            greatest
darkness

How can I bring my darkness
to my light and my light to
my darkness?

Give an example of each.

We become
that which
we resist

Think about how this happens.

Strong onesidedness creates
its opposite.

What is a personal example of this?

# ❀ A GREAT AFFIRMATION ❀

A great
                    affirmation
is to accept
                    denial


How can I feel positive when
someone denies me something?

Rehearse this. Act it out!

# ❀ A BLESSING ❀

May all our
　　　　obstacles
become bridges
　　　　to
the other side

List some present obstacles and
how they can be made into bridges.

Blaming is the
avoidance
of
suffering

I blame others because . . . ?

# ❀ THE BLIND ❀

In darkness
the blind make
the best guides

What truth is here for you?

# ❀ THE WOMB OF NEW BIRTH ❀

The shadow
is the womb
of new birth

The shadow is that side of myself
which I reject.

What in this side of myself needs,
and holds the seeds for, new birth?

## ❀ DISSENSION ❀

Unity
    breeds
dissension

When things are going well
be prepared for what?

Anger purifies
us to be real.

What do I need to do to creatively
accept anger in myself and others?

To affirm
meaning is
to transform
darkness


In my own words, the meaning of
my life comes out of doing what?

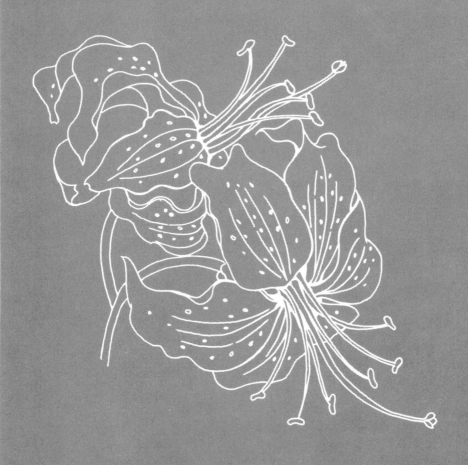

# ❀ Productivity ❀

Whether we know it consciously or not, one of the main things we want in life is to become more and more effective.

Picture the small child, ourselves, struggling to handle her parents, his body, her utensils, his relationships, and so on. Then into adult years, first taking the lowest paying jobs or having relationships with those who are not quite able to fully appreciate us.

Gradually we can grow in consciousness and effectiveness. Through experience and insight we learn more and more the way things really work in the world. We can comprehend, also, the way we each function and develop as persons.

And so productivity, the process of our being effective in life. Certainly we can measure ourselves by our accomplishments as well as our hopes for a fuller future?

May our accomplishments be varied and well worth the work they require. May they also reflect our deepest values and who we are really meant to be.

I am less swayed by who you say you are and what you would like to do than by what you have actually produced out of yourself into life. The arena of the world is reality and that is truly the place for each one of us to continually test our effectiveness.

Let us then elevate meaningful productivity to a high place in the spiritual hierarchy of things! It may happen in the most ordinary and basic of circumstances and it can happen at the truly great moments of our lives.

# ❄ ACTION ❄

Action is
the true test
of reflection

How would you contrast
reflection and action?

How many "no's"
does it take
to affirm
your "yes"?

This week why not test yourself by
going after something meaningful which
you really want and seeing how many
"no's" you collect until you get to
your "yes"?

# ❀ TO WANT WHAT YOU GET ❀

The best way
to get what you want
is to want
what you get

How can you learn more to want
what you get?

What are some of the destructive
ways you resist what comes your
way in life?

What will you do about them?

## ❀ TIME ❀

One cannot
save time
One can only
spend it wisely

What switch in attitude
is being asked for here?

## ❀ SUCCESS ❀

Success is
knowing the laws of
reality
and using them
effectively to
achieve one's goals

Success is what for you?

# ❀ THE REWARD ❀

Effectiveness
        is always rewarded
   with
   more responsibility

Am I ready for this?

What are my fears?

To whom
     much is given
         is much
    also required

Nobody said it would be easy.

How strong is your commitment?

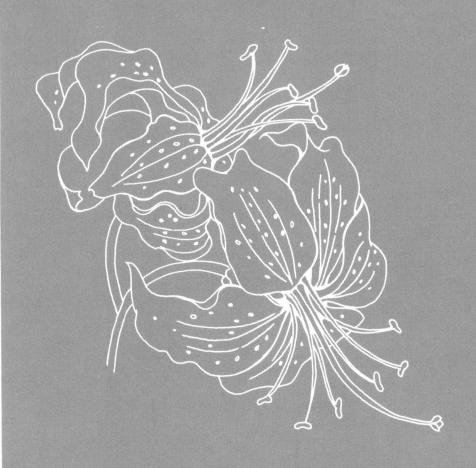

# ❁ Comic Relief ❁

Nothing is true unless the heart makes it so. If you are too serious about a thing chances are you are identified with it and therein can lie a kind of downfall. Identification breeds inflexibility. You will not be able to choose the new alternative if you are still stuck in the old one.

Along comes humor to jar us out of our identifications. We laugh when something goes wrong in life, when things do not work the way they are rationally meant to work.

Some of us cry or become angry when imperfections sneak up on us. Then again, others of us can move on to laughter also. We see in a flash the absurdity of the thing, the event, and make our adjustments.

Work is when we are identified with what we do. Play is when we are not identified with what we do. We just do it and see what happens.

In the same way humor frees us from ourselves. We recognize the broken or changed connection and we laugh. Without that laugh we would be identified with the intervention and then all life would become a total tragedy and even laughter would hurt.

We must begin to bid each other adieu, goodbye, have a rewarding journey. What better way than to disidentify from the form, the statements of principles, and the work we have been doing?

In the end I can offer you nothing, if not a paradox. What is real is also unreal. The best responses are responses of the heart.

❀ TIME ❀

Time

 screws us

 all

What does the word "screw" mean to you?

# ❀ CABBAGE SOUP ❀

Cabbage
　　　　soup
　　is
best
　　served
　　　　hot

What is real about this statement?

To get where
        you are
going
you must travel

In what senses is this
statement obvious?

What you do
      not know
is new
          knowledge

This must be saying something . . . ?

It is better
to be
profound
than stupid

Is it?

Humor
       is
           a
fast
exit

Goodbye!

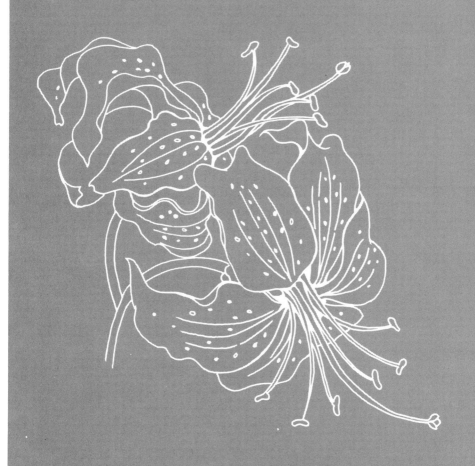

# ❀ Epilogue ❀

You have read them once, perhaps many more times than once. What do you think? How do you feel?

Our basic assertion is simple enough. That there are inherent laws as to the way life and reality work. And that through consciousness and experience we can begin to know these laws which we formulate here as principles and aphorisms.

To become centered and effective in life we have got to get our principles straight. This is our purpose and our task.

What resolution as ending can we offer each other now?

None but that we live what we share. We can be known in the journey. There is a bond, a fellowship, in the spirit and ground of things.

This is not the metaphor of poems written in bark floating down streams into oblivion. We want to make more than a gesture regarding life. We want to live it passionately and give it its full regard. This is not life as a metaphor for reality. This is life. This is reality. We are involved. We are committed whether we like it or not.

My heart goes forward like fire spreading through the lower branches and underbrush of a forest. First the burning and next the Springtime and new birth built on the ashes of the old.

In ending
evoke



beginning